Collected Minutes

from the

BAD MOTHERS'
MEETINGS

Collected Minutes from the Bad Mothers' Meetings by Annemarie Fleming

First published by Jane Curry Publishing 2015
[Wentworth Concepts Pty Ltd]

PO Box 780, Edgecliff, NSW 2027
AUSTRALIA

www.janecurrypublishing.com.au

National Library of Australia Cataloguing-in-Publication entry

Author: Fleming, Annemarie.

Title: The Collected Minutes of the Bad Mothers' Meetings / Annemarie Fleming

ISBN: 978-1-925183-06-1 (hbk.)

Subjects: Humour, Gift, Parenting

Editor: Amanda Hemmings

Cover design: Cheryl Collins Design

Cover illustrations: David Logan

Printed in China by Jade Productions

Production: Jasmine Standfield

Collected Minutes

from the

BAD MOTHERS' MEETINGS

Annemarie Fleming

To my gorgeous parents
Nana Mouskouri and Hazza Bajan.

And to my precious babies
Georgie, Sophia, Evangeline and Will
— with apologies.

The most remarkable thing about my mother was that for 30 years she served the family leftovers. The original meal has never been found.

Calvin Trillin

One Minute

An emergency meeting was held last night. The minutes follow:

The purpose of the meeting was to discuss Christmas gifts received and to provide strategies for dealing with said gifts.

One mother said that she had received a necklace which could best be described as looking like something you might pull out from under a car bonnet. Unfortunately her reaction on receiving the gift had been so genuinely gracious that she was now

1

required to wear the necklace to all social functions and — never mind the looks she was getting from family and friends — she was also staring down the barrel of some hefty physio bills due to the strain the thing was putting on her neck.

A suggestion was made to lose the necklace and blame it on a faulty clasp. The mother said that this was something she had tried, but had been unsuccessful as one of the children had found the necklace in the garden and (after much elation) her husband had promptly soldered the clasp shut so it was now impossible to undo.

After a general discussion involving burglaries, house fires and murder, it was decided that a life-threatening allergic reaction to the metal in the necklace was the best course of action. A coffee date was organised for the following morning during which time the medical emergency would take place. Stories were practised so all mothers were in sync re their description of the chain of events, including the bit about the doctor who was so intrigued by the case that he had organised for the necklace to be sent to Melbourne for scientific testing.

Another mother reported that she had received a gift with a twist this Christmas. Apparently a goat had been delivered on her behalf to an African village on Christmas Eve. The goat was then slaughtered for the village to feast upon. The twist was that the spirit of the goat was due to arrive at her house sometime between Christmas and New Year to provide bountiful feelings of goodwill.

All mothers present were intrigued and wanted to know whether the mother in question had noticed any difference in the atmosphere of the house. The mother said yes, she had definitely noticed a change. Since Christmas day, the dishwasher had packed it in, a dead rat and three live funnel-webs had been found in the pool and a candle had exploded leaving one child requiring stitches to the index finger.

At this point the mothers were stumped for a course of action. Visitors are bad enough — but ones you can't see — well that's just asking for trouble.

Meeting closed 10.35pm.

Bloody Norah

- 1 tablespoon salt
- 1/4 lemon, cut into two wedges
- 1/2 teaspoon Worcestershire sauce
- 1/4 teaspoon soy sauce
- 1/2 teaspoon freshly ground black pepper
- dash cayenne pepper
- 1/4 teaspoon hot sauce
- 1 teaspoon horseradish
- 2 measures vodka
- 4 measures tomato juice
- 1 stick celery

Place salt in a saucer. Rub rim of highball glass with a lemon wedge and coat in salt. Place lemon wedge on rim of glass and put some ice in the glass. Put the glass in the fridge if you can find room. Place Worcestershire, soy, black pepper, cayenne pepper, hot sauce and horseradish in a cocktail shaker. Fill shaker with ice and add vodka, tomato juice and juice of remaining lemon wedge. Shake vigorously. Taste for seasoning and heat, and adjust as necessary. Strain into chilled ice-filled glass. Garnish with celery stalk and serve immediately if not sooner.

My Day On a Plate

Breakfast. Arrive home from brisk morning walk feeling very thirsty. Make note to self that tonight will be alcohol free. Open fridge to find empty bottle of orange juice. Go for cereal option. Just about to pour milk when I remember that all school uniforms are still wet in machine. Make mad dash to the laundry and put clothes in dryer. Return to kitchen to find sleepy child eating my cereal and complaining that he can't find his uniform. Make school lunches. Take clothes out of dryer and iron them as dry as I can. As I run out the door to do school drop off, I remember I haven't had breakfast. Grab a handful of Chicken Crimpies and wash them down with red cordial.

✎

Lunch. Meet up with another mother on my lunch break so she can counsel me re the haircut I had on Saturday. She bursts out laughing when she sees me. Realise the double takes people

have been doing have been in a bad way, not a good way. Make note to self that late 40s is too late to get a fringe. Tell her if she thinks it looks bad now you should see it after eight hours sleep and that my husband now wakes up next to the love child of Rod Stewart and Suzi Quatro. She laughs so hard she spills a full coffee over my ham salad wrap, turning it into ham salad crap.

✍

Dinner. Rush to supermarket with no idea what to cook for dinner. Look around for inspiration and catch the eye of a smug cupcake mum who has just popped in for a few bits and pieces. Grab a small basket, just like hers, and proceed to do a full trolley shop. End up at checkout with two dislocated shoulders, bruising to the hip and kicking a large packet of toilet paper in front of me. Arrive home and realise that despite buying half the store I'm still not sure what's for dinner. Cut up an onion and throw it in a fry pan with some olive oil in the hope this will stop inevitable dinner menu questions. Look at clock. Smile. It's after five (in Fiji). Reach for wine glass. Remember alcohol-free promise. Frown. Put wine glass back. Start dinner (spag bol). Field dirty look from one child re I'm not sure what. Read note thrust in face from another child re urgency about bringing in four items by tomorrow for a chain reaction experiment. Assist Year 8 child with a maths problem involving compound interest, a man named Stacy and a waterbed purchase. Reach for wine glass...

My mother is about five foot with her hair done. Without it, she's about four foot ten.

Ryan Kwanten

Two Minutes

This is a special bulletin to all mothers to fill them in on the details of the annual Back to School Meeting which took place this week. Attendance was high due to residual New Year's Resolutions which were discussed at length. Apart from attending more meetings, one mother said that on New Year's Day she'd vowed to be less judgemental and eat more fish. Apparently since then, she's never been so judgemental in her life and she's been ordered out of the communal eating area at work.

First and foremost, book covering was discussed and how best to avoid excessive violence and swearing, accidental forearm waxing and binge drinking when in contact with Contact. Some excellent ideas came forward, including the Emperor's New Clothes technique where you send the books back uncovered and tell the child/teacher that they are actually covered in a very fine, state-of-the-art Contact. One mother who experimented with a range of Contacting techniques has discovered that the rim of a wine glass is much better at smoothing the bubbles than a ruler, and in keeping with the theme also suggested that a couple of bottles of bubbles makes the whole experience a lot more enjoyable and easier to forget the next day. As a result of the discussion, a Contact support group was set up. For details of the next meeting of the 'Run For Cover' group please see the President.

With the advent of parent/teacher information evenings, there was some discussion on how best to look interested when you're sitting at a child's desk listening to a summary of the Year

Four curriculum and it's past wine o'clock. Neck craning was advised to make it look like you really want to see the final line of the PowerPoint presentation. General interest in what is hanging up in the classroom was also recommended, although one mother advised not to comment too loudly or laugh out loud at any particular piece as, chances are, you'll be sitting next to the author's/artist's parents.

As usual, school lunches were discussed and it was noted that allergies — once the curse of the mother — are now actually working in our favour. With more and more foods appearing on the banned list, it seems that all children will be back to Vegemite sandwiches before you can say "ricotta and corn wrap". A general feeling of relief was evident at this point as all mothers present realised they finally had a comeback to those children who have, until now, been brandishing lavash bread and exotic dips in front of their own children.

Unless anything untoward happens at the parent information nights, the next meeting is scheduled for just before Easter — a time when cupcake mums turn us all into hot cross buns.

Meeting closed 12.04am.

Ma's Teary

- *2 measures gin*
- *1 measure dry vermouth*
- *1 dash of something bitter (tears OK)*
- *twist of lemon*
- *1 olive*

Combine ingredients in a mixing glass and fill with ice. Stir well to chill and strain into a chilled cocktail glass. Place a twist of lemon over the drink as garnish. If you can find an olive in the fridge, toss it in.

Chaos

Most mornings in my house are chaotic. Some are more chaotic than others. Our chaos runs from mild to moderate to severe. Mild chaos usually involves me quickly finishing off some Year Four homework, a drycleaning routine to remove a two-week-old banana from someone's school bag and a school run U-turn to collect a forgotten school project, hat, library book or lunch. Moderate chaos has all of the above ingredients as well as some sort of human disaster, eg, a suspected broken ankle, a hair knot that only a neurosurgeon can release or the sudden arrival of a suspicious-looking rash. Elements of a severely chaotic morning are not as predictable. The events that unfold on a severely chaotic morning are so bizarre that they fall into the same category as once-in-forty-year weather conditions. What I find most scary about the severely chaotic morning is that there are no predictors to alert you to its imminent arrival. Just like the calm before the storm, it starts out quite relaxed — like the one I had recently where I looked in disbelief at the clock.

Seven forty-five and everyone was ready. This was unheard of. I looked around suspiciously. Children breakfasted. Check. Girls dressed for school. Check. Lunches made. Check. Lunches packed. Check. Hair done. Check.

I went to find the pre-schooler. He was having his first kindergarten orientation morning today in preparation for the big day. On any other morning he may have decided to turn into Bear Grylls or Indiana Jones — characters that require rope belts and knives tucked into their shorts. But not today. Today he had taken my offering of a pair of shorts and a T-shirt without argument. There had been no request for me to plait some reeds from the garden so that he could wear them around his head or waist. Or to make a cardboard shark's tooth so he could wear it around his neck. He'd even agreed to wear underwear. I breathed a sigh of relief. Sure he was still in his pyjamas and the clothes were on the bed, but he'd agreed to wear them and I knew that he was true to his word. "Come on," I said. "Time to get dressed. We don't want to be late for orientation day."

I looked myself up and down. I was also showered and dressed. And I'd had breakfast. I breathed a sigh of relief. Seemed like this whole getting to school before the bell routine was becoming a little easier.

"I want the girls to dress me," said the pre-schooler.

He was sitting in his bedroom with his back turned, playing Lego. I smiled. Perhaps he was feeling nervous. As I went to find the girls, I thought what a lovely thing it was that he was asking his sisters for help.

"Girls, can you come and dress Will?" I called.

I looked around for any other potentially chaotic starting points. Handbag. Check. Car keys. Check. School newsletter? Was there a hat parade or a teddy bears' picnic or a crazy hair day that had slipped my mind? I skimmed the contents of the newsletter. No, nothing. Just an ordinary Thursday and it was eight o'clock and everyone was almost ready to get in the car. And then I heard the words that would send my morning careering out of control, like a car with no brakes plunging off a cliff.

"Mum, we can't get him dressed. He's locked himself in his handcuffs."

My immediate thoughts were positive. We'd only bought the handcuffs two days ago so the keys to unlock them couldn't be too lost. And they were plastic handcuffs, so I was sure I could cut them off if all else failed. I approached the problem with confidence.

"Do you know where the keys to the handcuffs are?" I asked him. He shook his head.

"Does anybody know where the keys to the handcuffs are?"

The girls shook their heads.

"OK, it's lucky we're early this morning. Everybody look for the keys. Sophia and Evie, you do the bedrooms. I'll have a look and see what else can be done."

While the girls searched, I took a look at the imprisoned pre-schooler's hands. He'd put them on fairly tight, making it impossible for me to gently wriggle his hands out of them. I got the scissors to see if I could cut through the plastic. After a couple of attempts, I gave up. Despite being classified as a toy, these cuffs were strong enough to restrain even the most hardened of villains. I made a trip to the tool box in the garage and found a pair of pliers and a screwdriver. I jiggled and filed and twisted. It was no good. The handcuffs were there to stay. I looked at my watch. We had to find the keys.

"Does anyone know where the keys are?" I said aloud as I shoved my hand into the nether regions of the couch.

My eldest daughter piped up. "I took the keys to Maddy's yesterday," she said sheepishly.

"Maddy's? Why did you take them to Maddy's?"

"We were playing a game."

I thought about asking what the game was, but there was no time and no point. I rang Maddy's mother.

"Bit of a strange request at 8.10 in the morning," I said. "Sophia left two small silver keys at your place yesterday. They're for Will's handcuffs. He's handcuffed himself and we can't unlock him. Does Maddy know where the keys are?"

"Can't you just cut them?"

"Tried that with scissors and pliers. They're made of really strong plastic."

"Can you pick them with a screwdriver?"

"Tried that. Didn't work. They're on quite tight and it hurts him if I jiggle them too much. We really need to find the keys."

"OK," said Maddy's mum. "We're on the job. I'll call you back."

Thirty seconds later the phone rang.

"Got them," came the jubilant voice down the line. Maddy's mum sounded as excited as someone who'd just found the Dead Sea Scrolls.

I let out a cry of joy. "Great! Can you bring them to school? Will's got his kindergarten orientation today. I can't get him dressed until I unlock him."

Maddy's mum let out a shriek of laughter. "I'll be there as soon as I can. We're running late. It's been one of those mornings."

Ten minutes later I was sitting in the car park at school waiting for the keys to arrive. I kept my head down to avoid eye contact with the stream of mothers who were walking their children into the school. One of them knocked on the car window, making me jump. I looked up. My heart sank. It was Claire. One of the perfect mothers who made her own playdough and always had cut up food in containers in case one of her children was about to die of starvation. She gestured for me to wind the window down.

"Is he nervous?" she said, pointing at Will in the back seat. She smelled strongly of sunscreen and common sense. I bet she'd never had a chaotic morning in her life.

"No, he's fine," I said, praying that she wouldn't notice that he was wearing a pyjama top and handcuffs.

She leaned in the window.

"Good luck, Will," she said. "Are you looking forward to big school?"

Will said nothing. And for the first time ever I didn't encourage a reply.

"We're just having a quiet moment before we go in," I said. Out of the corner of my eye, I could see Maddy's mum running towards the car holding the tiny keys in the air like a mad woman. I opened the car door on Claire to make her start walking. She was one of those people that didn't know how to say goodbye.

"I'll see you in there," I said. She smiled at me. A knowing smile that said, "I know he's your baby and you're sad about him starting school, but you really need to be strong and let him go."

God if she only knew.

Maddy's mum reached the car and handed me the keys. "I can't stay. I've got to get the car to the mechanics. Will you be OK?"

I gave her a quick kiss and a hug and she was gone. She had no problem with goodbyes.

I opened the back door. Will saw the keys and gave me a cheeky grin. He held his cuffed hands in the air. "I don't think Mrs Tannersaurus Rex would like these," he said.

Mrs Tanner, or Tannersaurus Rex as we liked to call her, was the head infants teacher. She was ancient and angry and enormous and I could just picture the condescending look that would arrive on her face if ever she did find out that Will had arrived at kinder orientation in a pyjama top and handcuffs. She would dine out on that story for months.

I leant in the car and unlocked one handcuff and then the other.

The girls screamed in delight at how easy it had been to get them off. Will rubbed his wrists. "I'm not doing that again," he said.

I looked at my watch. We still had five minutes before bell time. I took off Will's pyjama top and threw a T-shirt on him while the girls grabbed their bags. As we walked into the school grounds, I mentally reclassified the morning and downgraded it from severely chaotic to moderate. Perhaps I was getting better at handling the chaos. Looking back over the last half hour, I felt that I had handled the situation in a fairly cool manner. There had been no shouting, swearing or threats. I hadn't called an ambulance or a locksmith. I had been thrown into a tricky situation which I'd tackled head on and I'd come through with flying colours. This was a good thing. I had read recently that stress adds more deep-line wrinkles to your face than smoking or drinking and that adopting a calm approach can take years off. Perhaps I was looking younger than my 40 years.

I gave myself an invisible pat on the back as I kissed the girls and waved them goodbye. Nervous mothers and pre-schoolers mingled near the kindergarten classroom and Will and I walked over to join them hand in uncuffed hand. We mixed into the throng looking for all the world like a mother and son without a care in the world. Aside from a few red marks on Will's wrists, there were no signs of the drama that had unfolded half an hour ago.

We were welcomed into the classroom by Mrs Tannersaurus Rex. Will sat on the floor with the other children and I sat on a small chair at the back of the room with the other parents. I felt relaxed about Will starting school. I knew he was going to love it.

Mrs Tannersaurus Rex was putting on a great show. Any new parent to the school would come away from this morning thinking she was the sweetest woman they'd ever met. She was showing the children a craft activity and she invited the parents to accompany their child to a seat and help them with the activity and to leave the classroom as soon as they felt their child was comfortable.

"Don't hang about," she said in saccharine tones. "Your children are in good hands. We'll see you back here at twelve o'clock."

I crouched down next to Will and helped him glue some cotton balls onto a sheep.

"I'm going now," I said after a while, giving him a kiss.

"Bye Mum," he said.

As I walked from the classroom, I downgraded the morning from moderate to mild. Looking back, this morning had actually very little chaos in it at all. I was wrong to call it a chaotic morning. It had actually been quite calm.

I turned to wave at Will as I walked out the door but he had his eyes down, engrossed in his craft activity. The boy sitting next to him saw me waving and gave Will a shove.

"WILL, YOUR NANNA'S WAVING AT YOU!" he said at the top of his lungs.

And so began my severely chaotic morning.

I feel my mother about the place.
I don't think she haunts me,
but I wouldn't put it past her.

Julie Walters

Three Minutes

For those interested, the minutes of the last meeting follow:

Meeting opened at 7pm. All attendees arrived on time. One mother had to leave as soon as she got there due to a phone call from home informing her that both fridge doors had fallen off.

Past business. With Easter looming, a time that is traditionally a minefield of craft and cooking disasters for bad mothers everywhere, a suggestion was made that we should discuss last

Easter to try and prevent the same catastrophes this year. After a general discussion, a motion was put forward to move on. Sure, the evening could have been spent boiling the bunnies of Easters past and dissecting the disasters surrounding hat parades, egg blowing and live chicken hatchings but, as one mother so rightly said, "The little darlings have got to have something to talk about when they lie on the loopy lounge."

Guest speaker. We were fortunate to have a visiting guest speaker who has just written a book, *What Mother Is That? — A Field Guide*. It will no doubt become the bible for all bad mothers, especially the handy reference guide which helps to quickly identify mothers as well as giving tips on how to "get on" with the species subtypes.

A few examples follow:

"The Mother Superior." Physical description: nostrils slightly flared and a smug look on her face like she's smelling something she knows she shouldn't outwardly enjoy. Dress: organic cotton wraparound skirt in a retro print and Dutch footwear. Handy hint: if you find yourself engaged in conversation with a mother superior, keep it light. Although they look like someone you feel you could be friends with, they have very strong opinions and aren't afraid to voice them.

"The Cupcake Mum." Physical description: just like cupcakes, these women come in various shapes and sizes. Some are plain, some highly decorated. Many have a Tupperware cupcake carrier soldered to their left hand which makes identification easy. Handy hint: although this harmless species may charm you with their common sense and pipe-icing ability, try not to get frosty with them. These mothers are best kept on your good side at all times.

"The Stop-watch Mum." Physical description: These mothers come in only two sizes, XXS or XXXL. Dress: stretchy stuff for daywear and crushed-look stretchy stuff for evenings. Only interests are stop-watch times, carnival events, sports injuries and the best way to get to Bathurst for the weekend hockey trials. Handy hint: if you're struggling to strike up a conversation at school pick-up, make a beeline for a stop-watch mum. They will happily talk to anyone who'll listen about what times their children did at the latest athletics meet.

Meeting closed at 11.31pm with all mothers purchasing the book and wondering when **What Mother Is That?** *will appear as an app.*

Ma's Greeter

- *3/4 cup lemon juice*
- *3/4 cup lime juice*
- *3 1/2 cups good-quality tequila*
- *2 cups Cointreau, Grand Marnier or Triple Sec*
- *1/2 cup sugar syrup (or more to taste)*
- *ice cubes*
- *salt*

Combine all ingredients in punch bowl and stir. Serve immediately in salt-rimmed glasses filled with ice.

NB: The recipe quantities are for group not individual use.

Is Laughter Really the Best Medicine?

Whoever coined the phrase "laughter is the best medicine" obviously hadn't had abdominal surgery. I admit it's a phrase I've used myself on many occasions to tend to those around me who have ailed at one point or another. And more often than not, I've been the first to dole out the "medicine"...a joke about a farmer and his bad sex life, a funny story about something that happened on the weekend or a witty character appraisal... I am up there with the best of them, dishing out the humour in extra large tablespoons. Until now. Now I am laid up in bed with a large slice across my tummy held together by who knows how many internal stitches. Phrases like "side splitting" and "gut wrenching" have taken on a new meaning. Any sort of stomach muscle movement hurts. The thought of a belly laugh fills me with terror.

By the time the children arrive to visit me, I have pressed the button on the lovely self-serve pethidine drip so many times that the nurse has scheduled me in for an appointment with a counsellor from Drug and Alcohol. But I don't care, the pain has gone.

"How is everyone?" I grin as the children walk through the door.

"Good," they say, looking at me weirdly.

"What's wrong with you Mum?" asks my youngest.

"I'm fine," I say, trying to focus so he has only one face. "Why?"

"You look strange," he says. "Are you on drugs?"

"No," I say defensively, like he's the parent and I'm the child. I push the button under the sheets. "I mean yes, yes, of course I'm on drugs. I've just had my uterus taken out." The children glare at me to try and stop me talking. Which of course has the opposite effect. "Apparently it was the biggest uterus the doctor has ever seen," I say, trying to sound serious.

"Ewwww," says a teenager. "Spare us the details."

"Well, it's all very well to say 'Ewww', but without my 'Ewwwterus', *you* all wouldn't be here." I burst out laughing at how funny I am. The pain returns and I clutch my tummy. The children stare at me blankly.

"You forgot to send in the money for the sushi workshop," says the youngest.

The words sushi and workshop in the same sentence are too much for me to bear. "Sushi workshop," I splutter. "What the hell is a sushi workshop?"

"Sensei is going to show us how to make sushi," says the child.

"Oh is she now? Well if sensei says sushi then sensei it is." A silence descends as the children process the thought that their mother is off her face. "I think we'll go now," says the eldest, herding the others to the door.

"OK," I grin. "Have a lovely time at the sushi workshop." I burst out laughing, clutch my sides and, as they leave the room, I am struck by the fact that a hysterectomy is like a caesarean but without the responsibility. A gratefulness descends upon me which I play around with for a while as I watch the clock to check when I can push the button again.

The next day, the drip is ripped from me. I snatch desperately at the magic button as the nurse pulls it from my grasp. She throws me a couple of Panadol and runs from the room. I lie there suffering from having the largest uterus in the world cut out of me and gradually the pain kicks in.

My sisters visit. I am pleased to see them. But I've forgotten. They are the Physicians of Laughter. In their presence, I am a mere intern. It starts with a quick-witted quip from my older sister about one of the nurses. I clutch at my tummy. "Please don't make me laugh," I say. "It hurts and I don't want to burst my stitches." The atmosphere sobers. They sit. We look around, searching for something, anything, to say that isn't funny. This in itself is funny. We start to giggle. "You're going to have to go!" I say. "You're making me laugh." "But we're not saying anything," they protest. "Well, unless you can talk about something completely serious," I reply, trying to keep a straight face, "you're going to have to go." Silence again. My younger sister stands up. "We'll come back tomorrow," she says. As they disappear out the door, I can hear them gut laughing in the hospital corridor. I begin to laugh at the thought of the sight of them. The pain is unbearable. I feel like I'm going to split open. I try to think of something serious. Sick people. Dead people. Sad stories. The laughter inside me slowly subsides.

As the days go on, and more of the family phone or visit, I am struck by the realisation that I come from a family of clowns — unable to have a serious conversation about anything. I yearn to come from a long line of boring people who sit quietly and talk in hushed tones about the difference in petrol prices between here and the outskirts of Sydney, or the plans they have to build a double garage, or some documentary they saw on the GFC. Over the next few days, as I venture out into the corridors, I look longingly at the visitors that the other patients are receiving. Serious, concerned faces. There is no bedside laughter.

My room on the other hand is like the casting office for a comedy festival. The air is filled with funny stories about yoga classes and hairdressers and workmates. Puns punctuate, wit whirls and repartee resounds. I have no line of defence. I try to laugh just with my mouth, like a Cheshire cat, to take the pressure off my tummy muscles, but it doesn't help. In the end, I tell them all to go! I put a "No Visitors" sign on my door and resign myself to the fact that I will not be able to see any of them for at least six weeks. As I lie back, I think of my mum and I remember the time when she'd had surgery and we went to visit her. During the visit, intrigued by the hospital band around

44

her wrist, I leant over to read it aloud. "Shoe repair?" I said. My mother clutched at her stomach. "Schumaker," she said, trying desperately not to laugh. "It says Schumaker. The doctor's name is Schumaker." She tried to shift the topic to something vaguely serious. But it was too late. My father and four siblings were doubled over at the thought of someone going to hospital to have a shoe repaired. I remember her ordering her family out, like I have just done. I begin to smirk at the thought of it. The smirk turns to a grin. I can't help it. I begin to giggle. The giggle becomes more serious. I can feel it heading down to my stomach muscles to gather force so it can become a laugh. My head is filled with images of shoes and hospitals and doctors who are cobblers and people going to operating theatres to have a sole replaced. It's no good. I start to laugh. When I finally calm down the tears in my eyes are from pain, not laughter. I scold myself that I should have known better. I should have included myself on the list of banned people at the door. To stop myself laughing, I think of sad movies — Sophie's Choice, Love Story, Terms of Endearment. The urge to laugh recedes.

And then I start thinking about titles of movies that would suit my own predicament — The Year My Uterus Broke springs to mind. I smile broadly. The smile becomes a snigger. The snigger becomes a laugh. I clutch my tummy and wince in pain. It's going to be a long six weeks...

Living with a teenage daughter
is like living with the Taliban:
a mum is not allowed to laugh,
sing, dance or wear short skirts.

Kathy Lette

Four Minutes

After a particularly harrowing start to the school year, a number of mothers surfaced recently. The minutes follow:

A general discussion re just what had made Term One so tumultuous revealed a common thread — school theme days — which now appear as a weekly event on many school calendars.

One mother reminisced about the time when a mufti day came around just once a year. Sure, she still hardly ever managed to remember to dress her children out of uniform, but she didn't feel she'd done too much damage if for just one day of the year they were the only ones adrift in a sea of My Little Pony and Bob the Builder outfits.

Another mother told the meeting her children had recently had a "No Rubbish Day", where all children were encouraged to bring their lunch to school without any wrapping. "What was I supposed to do?" she asked in exasperated tones. "Wrap the sandwiches in cheesecloth tied to sticks and send the children to school like a band of medieval wanderers?"

She ended up wrapping everything in plastic and telling her children they would get a slushy at the end of the day if they successfully hid the evidence — a manoeuvre that received a round of applause.

One mother said that she had been really knocked for six by an end of term "Cupcake Carnival". A note had come home asking for home-baked goods to be taken to school on Friday. The cakes were to be nut free, gluten free, dairy free and sugar free and they were not to be purchased from a store.

"I had trouble imagining what a nut-, gluten-, dairy- and sugar-free cake would even look like, let alone taste like," she said. All mothers present screwed up their noses in sympathy. It had taken a couple of years for us all to get a handle on the nut-free regime, but we'd really been hit hard by the gluten-free crisis (GFC).

The mother ended up solving the dilemma by keeping her child home from school that day. "I didn't want him to be around large quantities of zucchini and eggplant," she said. "He goes a bit funny around that sort of stuff."

Meeting closed 11.39am.

Side-Swiped

This one is perfect for those out of control days when you feel like someone has been driving you around at breakneck speed in a sidecar.

- *2 measures cognac*
- *1 measure Cointreau*
- *fresh lemon juice, to taste*
- *orange or lemon peel (maybe)*
- *superfine sugar, for garnish (optional)*

Prepare the cocktail glass by running some lemon juice around the rim, then dip the rim in sugar. Chill the glass. Combine all the ingredients in an ice-filled cocktail shaker. Shake well and pour into glass. Taste and adjust, adding more lemon juice if necessary and garnish with a twist of orange or lemon peel if you can be bothered.

The Mumectomy

Sometimes it is in the best interest of the child to have a mother removed — an intricate surgical procedure known as a mumectomy. Unfortunately, by the time a child is identified as needing a mumectomy, the mother is often quite firmly planted in the child and has laid down a root system more intricate than the underground sewer system of London. For this reason, mumectomies generally have a low success rate as regrowth is common. Having said this, children who survive the operation with the mother completely removed do go on to live often quite remarkable lives.

As an example, let's look at Andy Murray — the perennial bridesmaid — always holding up the runners-up trophy with that grim Scottish look on his face that cries out, "Take pity on me. I need a mumectomy." But during the last couple of years, Andy's luck has begun to change and he's started to win a tournament or two. So what's happened? Well, while it hasn't been

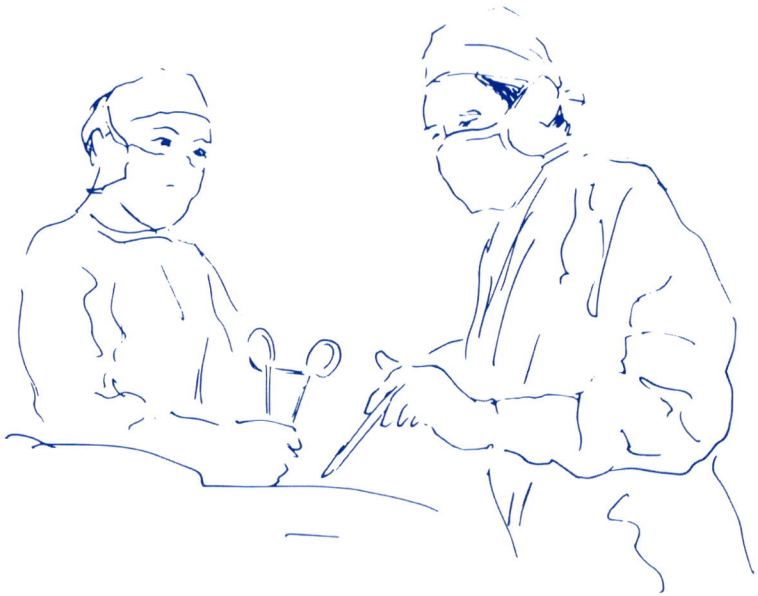

confirmed, I believe his coach is in the process of performing what looks like being a very successful mumectomy.

It used to be that the only people in Andy's box at major matches were his mother and one or two stray uncles. But just lately, someone else has taken up residence — a very beautiful girlfriend. Sure the mother is still there — hands clenched around her own throat — but nowadays when Andy loses a point and looks up to his box for support, his eyes go straight to the very beautiful girlfriend. It's not rocket science to realise that this must be a whole lot more encouraging than taking in the pain and desperation that radiates from his mother's face.

Although not as common, another procedure called the dadectomy is sometimes performed. Once again, if we study the tennis world, a number of examples pop up — Jelena Dokic, Steffi Graf, and Jennifer Capriati just to name a few. All struggled with their careers at one point or another due to the stranglehold their dads had on them. Some have had successful dadectomies and gone on to win a few matches. Others haven't been so lucky.

And then, there's Lleyton Hewitt. If he wants to start winning, he needs a double parentectomy. But he also needs to know that the success rate for this operation is incredibly low. And I, for one, don't hold out much hope.

I want my children to have all
the things I couldn't afford.
Then I want to move in with them.

Phyllis Diller

Five Minutes

For those who missed the last meeting, here are the minutes:

Attendance: seven mothers. Most arrived late. All smelt of cab sav or sem sav blanc. No apologies.

Meeting opened with the pledge: "We acknowledge we are all bad mothers. We don't organise play dates. We don't chop food into small pieces and carry it around in case someone gets the munchies. We can't find a lid to fit any container in the house. We don't soak, fold or iron. We vacuum the bath. We acknowledge we are all bad mothers but we're doing our bloody best."

New Business

Birthday parties. All agreed this was an area of contention. A motion was put forward that if it is absolutely necessary to have a party, i.e., if said child is turning 12 and has never had one before, that the party should be of one hour duration with no themes, home-baked goods, party bags, piñatas, or games involving prior planning. All in favour. No objections. Motion carried.

School canteens. General discussion re the demise of the party pie and sausage roll. Acknowledgement that they have been replaced by low fat varieties, but as one mother expressed, "For God's sake, the little buggers have got to have a bit of fat in their diet." Another mother expressed concern re how long it was taking to write out the lunch order onto the brown paper bag, e.g.,

"One Crunchy Munchy Salad, no cherry tomatoes, and one serve of fresh seasonal fruit." Discussion regarding whether it may take less time to actually slap a bit of something on a piece of bread and wrap it up. All mothers agreed to try this at least once before the next meeting and report back with results.

School pick-up zone. All mothers expressed relief that most schools were now offering a drive-through service. Some schools, however, are still stuck in the dark days of the walk-in-pick-up and those mothers required strategies on how to avoid the cupcake mums. Advice ranged from pretending you have the mumps, to wearing a disguise, to being in a hurry. One mother admitted that the last option was probably not the best because she'd recently dislocated her child's shoulder. Another suggested that feigned illness didn't always work because in all likelihood a cupcake mother would drop a meal around and catch you finishing off a bottle of wine and a box of BBQ Shapes whilst you cooked dinner.

Other business. A suggestion was made that a Christmas Support Group be set up. This idea was enthusiastically received and a meeting planned for early December. Suggested agenda items include: how to make an elf suit in five minutes out of the felt you've ripped out of your grandmother's dresser, rehearsing a polite response to "Have you finished all your shopping?" and practising how to swig discreetly from the bottle that you've smuggled into the Christmas concert.

Meeting closed 10.32pm.

I Rush Coffee

- *2 measures Irish whiskey*
- *4 measures freshly brewed coffee*
- *dash of brown sugar syrup*
- *whipped cream*

Pre-warm a mug with hot water. Add whiskey, syrup and coffee. Stir to combine, and gently spoon a more than generous dollop of cream on top. Note: this coffee is best left until after the school run.

The Spray Tan

My skin summer range comes in two colours — red or white. For me, a golden tan is just a pigment of my imagination. And I know that pale skin can be very fetching on some people — like Cate Blanchett or Naomi Watts — but my pale skin is a whiter shade of pale. Seen in its full glory, it's enough to make one gasp in wonder or fall about hysterically laughing. I have tried in the past to apply fake tans myself and always ended up looking as if someone had thrown two brown squash balls at my knees with full force — so I decided to go to the beauticians and get a spray tan. A couple of pointers:

Do make sure you tell the children what you're doing. I left the house looking like Snow White and returned in a kaftan, looking like Kamahl. "What's happened to you Mum?" one child asked. "Your legs are like mud."

It's also a good idea to lock the children in their rooms when you come back from getting the tan. This not only spares them from watching you go gradually darker and darker, but chances are if you let them out, one of them will have some sort of mishap involving water: a precious toy dropped into the pool that has to be retrieved immediately, a serious spillage that requires a major clean up or a child covered in something toxic — these situations are best avoided until after you've showered to prevent yourself looking like a brown and white striped marsupial.

Also, don't book the appointment for six o'clock when you have guests coming for dinner at seven. It wasn't until I was baring all in bikini bottoms, standing with arms outstretched like a paper doll in a chain, that the beautician told me the bronzer would darken gradually over the next two hours after which time I could shower and wash it off to uncover the "natural tan". I did a quick calculation. This would mean I would have to excuse myself after the guests arrived...so I made the fateful decision not to shower until after they had left. As a result, my guests were greeted by someone with a healthy bronzed glow and farewelled by someone who looked like she'd been out fighting fires for a couple of weeks. At ten o'clock, the light bulb blew in the gazebo and my guests were unable to contain their laughter as they were guided back through the garden and into the house by the whites of my eyes. What did I do? Well, there was nothing else to do except break into a rendition of "Golden Brown" and really make them laugh.

"Mothers don't have headaches.
They have SPLITTING headaches.
Do you think screaming for
nine hours a day has anything
to do with it?"

Jerry Seinfeld

Six Minutes

An extraordinary meeting was held at the weekend to wet Prince George's little head. The minutes are as follows.

All mothers in attendance arrived with a bottle of champers. As we downed the first glass and looked forward to the next, we began to reminisce about the early days of our own first born. By the end of the second glass some pearls of wisdom emerged and some advice on lessons learned.

One mother said she had initially struggled with the whole concept of the mother's bag — not only remembering to bring it with her when she left the house, but also what to put in it so she looked like she knew what she was doing. Apart from nappies and wipes, she had never discovered what other mothers put in their bags, which was a bit of a mystery because their bags always seemed full to the brim. She told us that one day she'd gone to mothers group with a bag stuffed with a DVD player wrapped up in a couple of her husband's workshirts. She'd had the morning from hell — she'd lost the keys, then found them in the bin, the phone had been chain ringing and the washing machine had nearly walked out the door. By the time she got to the car and realised that nobody had had breakfast, she did what any normal, sane mother would do, which was to take the poor excuse for a mother's bag she was carrying and take it back into the house and stuff it with whatever she could get her hands on. Then she topped it off with the necessary requirements — nappies, wipes, drinks and food. Arriving at the mothers group, she was greeted with looks of admiration as she lugged the straining canvas bag through the door. Lesson learned: the bigger the bag, the better the mother.

Another mother said she wished she had been warned about the plastics drawer in the kitchen — an obvious hive of reproductive activity and polyethylene morphing. She hadn't even intended to have a plastics drawer, but she had mistakenly thrown together a Tupperware container and a drink bottle one night and by morning the drawer was crammed with plates, cups, bottles and containers, none of them with matching lids. Lesson learned: keep your plastics apart.

Another mother advised to choose your audience carefully before sharing any of the brilliant inventions you come up with in the night while walking a baby to keep it asleep. Hers included a detachable arm, so she could put the baby down without it knowing, and removable exterior shoulder pads, so she didn't have to smell of formula vomit all day. She admitted to being so taken with the shoulder pad idea that she had a few made up in an assortment of trendy terry towelling patterns, and had taken them to one of the many mothers groups that she had tried to be part of. Suffice to say they did not take on. Lesson learned: mothers groups, schmothers groups.

Meeting ended just before dawn.

Gin Fizz

When everything's fizzing all around you, get a bit fizzy with it yourself!

- *2 measures gin*
- *1 measure cream*
- *1 egg white*
- *1/2 measure lemon juice*
- *1/2 measure lime juice*
- *2 teaspoons sugar, to taste*
- *soda water*

Combine everything except the soda water in a blender and whizz on high for 10 seconds until foamy. Place mixture in a cocktail shaker laden with ice and shake for 20 seconds. Strain into a chilled glass and add soda to taste.

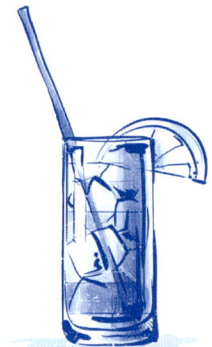

My Left Shoe

Shopping for shoes or clothes with children is like trying to herd cats. It's very hard to keep one eye on them and one on the racks — and it always seems to be that while you're herding the cats, a lot of very nice things seem to appear on the racks. Inevitably as soon as you find something that you want to try on, one of the cats will need to go to the toilet. When you finally locate the toilets, you will try desperately to convince the other cats that they need to try to go as well because you're not making another visit. But of course none of the other cats need to go — until you've made your way back to the dressing room and have managed to squeeze yourself into a dress two sizes too small which you now can't get out of — at which point one of the other cats will need desperately to do a number two.

Recently the planets aligned and I had one child-free hour to check out the sales at a large department store. Like a lioness on the prowl, I stalked quickly through the women's fashion

department and was disappointed (but not surprised) that the racks held nothing that interested me at all. I headed to the shoe department — which was where I spotted it — out of the corner of my eye — something special. Leopard print. Not just any leopard print mind you. These leopard print flats were very elegant in design. Not the cougar sort of leopard print you might find paired with some white slacks on the Gold Coast.

Moving in for the kill I quickly grabbed the shoe and tried it on. As luck would have it, it was exactly my size. Although it was flat, it had a nice rubber sole making it perfect for a luncheon date with a friend, but also equally at home on the sidelines at the Saturday morning soccer. I was a very hungry lioness now. I wanted the other one. I looked around. It was nowhere to be found. I went to the counter. The sales assistant was tall. As tall as a giraffe.

"I'd like to take these," I said, handing the left shoe over.

"Certainly, Madam. Did you manage to find the other one?"

"No," I said.

She set out across the plain to find it and I followed her. And then she stopped, mid-stride, like she'd just sensed danger. She turned to me and peered down. "I'm afraid there's a problem," she said. She pointed to a lady who was just slipping on my other shoe. I was momentarily taken aback. And then a piece of information that I have kept in my brain for more than 20 years made its way to my mouth.

"But the left shoe has the right of way," I blurted.

The shop assistant looked at me warily and raised her eyebrows. "I'm afraid I haven't heard that before." She strode off and tried unsuccessfully to camouflage herself behind a carousel of slippers.

I looked at the woman trying my shoe on. Surely she knew the rule. "Do you want to fight for it?" I said, trying to make light of a situation I could feel was going to turn nasty. She had ginger hair and she stared at me unblinking, like a meerkat. I tried to stare back, but her gaze didn't shift and I retreated, still clutching my half of the pair. I moved from table to table, casually picking up shoes as if I might find a shoe I liked better. As if. After a while I glanced over in her direction. Like a true meerkat, she remained, body stretched tall, head high, nose twitching, watching my every move. I ducked down and took refuge beside a lake of Jane Debsters.

And then it hit me. A brilliant plan! Hide the shoe and come back after I'd picked the kids up from school. I crawled commando-style across the plain, shoe tucked down the front of my top and I planted it, in the instant the meerkat looked away, in a pile of blue-striped loafers. I stood up, feigned some serious interest in an ankle boot and then blended into the crowd. In no time I was out of the department store and hightailing it home.

That afternoon I returned to the scene of the crime with the cats. I headed straight to the hiding spot and I couldn't believe it! The leopard print flat was still there! I've always found it amazing how leopards can camouflage so well. I took the shoe and headed over to find its partner. The meerkat had long gone. But so had the right shoe. That dirty meerkat. Had she hidden her shoe as well? I looked frantically through the piles but it was nowhere to be found. I went to the counter. This time I talked to a woman with a smile as wide as a zebra's. "Hi darl, how can I help?" she asked.

I explained that I'd like to take the leopard skin flats but I couldn't find the right shoe. "Just a minute, darl," she said. "I'll go and see if it's out the back." To my surprise, she returned with the box. "Here we go, darl!"

An internal chant of "I beat the meerkat! I beat the meerkat!" began within me. I smiled smugly as I handed over my credit card.

"Oh, hang on," said the zebra, face falling. "There's a note here. A lady has them on hold. Apparently she was in this morning and she couldn't find the other one."

I slunk out of the store, snarling with disappointed rage.

I have to keep reminding myself
that I am their mother. Sometimes
we're sitting at home and I feel
like we're waiting for our mum
to come home.

Ruby Wax

Seven Minutes

The inaugural book club was held last week, the first selected text being *Fifty Shades of Grey*.

One mother announced on arrival that she hadn't read the book because she's renovating and has spent the last two weeks with her head in a Dulux colour chart detailing 50 shades of birch. She just couldn't stomach the thought of delving headlong into another hue.

As the night progressed, another bad mother confessed to not having read the book but added that she felt she knew something about the story because she'd overheard a co-worker talking about it. She admitted feeling quite nostalgic when hearing about one of the main characters — an arrogant self-assured man named Christian who reminded her of a merchant banker from the North Shore with whom she'd had an on-again off-again relationship in her 20s. She then reminisced (in more detail than absolutely necessary) and concluded that if she were to write a memoir about the affair, it could be named *Fifty Lays in Gladesville*.

Spurred on by the frank monologue, another mother piped up to say that she also hadn't read the book but if she were to write a memoir about her promiscuous 20s, it would be *Fifty Strays I've Laid*.

To shift the topic another mother declared that she also hadn't read the set text because the only books she reads nowadays are cookbooks with either a number or the word "quick" in their title. She suggested that perhaps if the book had been called *Fifty Ways With Gravy*, in might have got more of a look in. Another mother added that given the amount of time her husband was spending at the local club a book named *Fifty Ways With a Meat Tray* would be more helpful.

With thoughts now turned to cooking, another bad mother — who also hadn't read the book — told us she had always wanted to write and photograph a coffee table book relating to food but she has now realised that she is no good at either cooking or photography, so she's given up on the idea. Someone replied that she shouldn't be deterred and that she should go ahead and detail her culinary disasters in a book to be titled *Fifty Plates That Went Astray*.

With all mothers now admitting to not having read the book a decision was made to scrap the book club idea and start a wine club, with the idea that we select and taste a different wine each month. An online order was placed on the spot — for 50 crates of chardonnay.

Meeting closed 11:08pm.

Sour Whiskers

This is a good antidote if you've been mixing with people with negative energy.

- *2 measures whiskey*
- *freshly squeezed lemon juice*
- *1 teaspoon sugar*
- *1 egg white (optional)*

Place ingredients into a cocktail shaker, fill with ice and shake for 10 seconds (a little longer if you've decided to use the egg white). Strain into a chilled glass of any size and garnish with the name of the sour whiskers who has annoyed you today.

Book Clubs

I have tried book clubs in the past. Three in total. None of them successful. Each has been like a love affair: intoxicating and breathless at the start, loyal and reliable as the months rolled on, and tedious and boring towards the end. The break-ups have never been easy. Excuses. Feigned illness. Untruths. In the end, to escape the tangled web I'd woven, I have had to fall back on George Costanza's favoured break-up line: "It's not you, it's me."

When I was asked to join another book club — Book Club Number Four — my answer was a fairly abrupt "no". But my refusal set me thinking about why it is that I haven't been able to stay the distance. Why have I not been able to settle into the relationship, as have so many book club members?

From the outside I look the part. I am a writer. I read. I love language and playing with words. I love chatting about authors and the stories they tell. I also enjoy a glass of wine and some camembert. Throw in a sense of humour and I'm looking like the perfect candidate. So perhaps my break-up line is wrong. Perhaps I should have said, "It's not me, it's you."

I now realise Book Club Number One was wrong from the start. Caught up in the heady days of my eldest daughter starting big school, the whole idea seemed attractive. A chance to meet other mums from the class. A night off from the family routine of teeth, bed and story. At our first meeting, we compiled a list of books we had enjoyed so we could plan what we would read and discuss in the coming months. *Girl With a Pearl Earring*, *My Sister's Keeper*, *Memoirs of a Geisha*. The list was a little too "bestseller" for my liking, but I didn't want to rock the boat.

The first few get-togethers were great. A couple of glasses of wine, a cheese plate and lots of reassuring discussion about all those little things I wondered whether I was doing right regarding school — e.g., bus pass applications, homework, what to pack in a lunchbox. But, as the months went by, cracks appeared. The book club meetings weren't as satisfying as I'd imagined they'd be. Why? I couldn't put my finger on it. And then one night on the way home, it hit me. We didn't discuss the book.

Book Club Number Two also involved mothers. I was not as green this time around. I questioned whether this was the right thing for me, considering my last experience. I was reassured that this was indeed a very "booky" book club and certainly the upcoming book, *Purple Hibiscus*, which had been short-listed for the Orange Prize, was definitely one I wanted to read. I was pleasantly surprised to find a list of discussion questions in my letterbox a week before our planned meeting, so I committed to going along just once to try it out.

The house was a mansion. The food was like something I'd never tasted before — cheese the host had driven two hours to pick up, shiraz from a private cellar that I was later taken on a tour of, and desserts that had arrived from an artisan bakery.

We did discuss the book, but I was so busy worrying about the second mortgage I'd have to take out to renovate the house and to feed and water these women in the manner they were accustomed to, when it came to my turn to be host, that I didn't take any of it in.

By the time I heard on the grapevine that Book Club Number Three was looking for a new member, I was hardened. I knew what I wanted: minimal wine — one glass, perhaps none even — and no food. No elaborate soft furnishings. Apart from greetings and farewells, I wanted no other chat — no stories about husbands or children. I wanted quite simply to discuss a book.

First impressions looked good. The club was run by a community group. There was a book list, so you knew what was coming up and as I scanned the titles, my heart began to race. *Wuthering Heights*, *The Brief Wondrous Life of Oscar Wao* — a mixture of classic and contemporary titles that took my breath away. It was held on the second Tuesday of each month in a rundown local hall. There was nothing soft about the furniture. In fact, you had to be early to score a rusty old folding chair. The people were from all walks of life.

When I reached my six-month anniversary, I still had no idea what any of them did for a living and I liked it that way. If I didn't show up one month, no one questioned where I was. Book Club Number Three was like a nonchalant lover who took you in and showed you a good time, but didn't blink an eye if you never came back again. So what went wrong?

Looking back, I can see that in Book Club Number Three's case, it was me, not them. Not that we ever had the break-up meeting. Three probably still hasn't realised that I'm not there. And I think that's what did my head in, in the end. It was too literary. I missed a bit of banter. I missed the glass of wine. I missed the laughter. Book Club Number Three took itself too seriously — there were too many discussions of fiction versus creative non-fiction and too much dissection of text.

So, what is my book club perfect match? I definitely need the book to be the focus. I'd like classics on the list, a Coonawarra shiraz in my glass and the company of people that I don't see on a social basis. I'd like the discussion to be mostly about the book, but with an interest in each other and a few laughs in between. Am I asking too much? Perhaps. But for the moment, I remain celibate and untempted.

I was so ugly, my mother
used to feed me with a slingshot.

Rodney Dangerfield

Eight Minutes

Due to an escalated interest in the mothers meetings which have been held on an irregular basis throughout the year, a mothers conference has been planned so that we can all sleep in the following morning. The conference will be held at an undisclosed location as a way of eluding any cupcake mums, Swedish sandal mums, sporty mums, mums suffering from excessive after school activity (EASA) syndrome or anyone else who might be under the misguided belief that they are bad mothers and that it might be good to go along for a laugh. No fakes allowed — this conference is for the genuine article. Handbags will be searched on entry. Any mother carrying a bag that does not contain multiple tissue-covered lollies, old notes that haven't made it to the class teacher, finger puppets, fluffy tampons, ticket stubs from movies that are now considered classics, whizzled up fruit and unknown keys will be refused entry.

The mothers conference will commence at midday Friday with a champagne lunch and the opportunity to listen to the guest speaker — a mother who has recently returned from a work-related conference in Western Australia. While she reports she doesn't remember a lot of what went on during her time in Perth, she does have two important items to relay as part of her keynote address — the first of these being the difference between placing a split bet vs a street bet on the roulette wheel and the other being how to communicate with Gen Y. I'm sure both topics will generate some interesting discussion and perhaps spark some ideas for placing your bets when it comes to communicating with any teenagers in the house.

Dinner will be served sometime after lunch. Following dinner a "school disco" dance-off will be held with prizes given for best imitation of the school principal, secretary, class teacher and librarian.

Accommodation will be in single rooms to alleviate any stress felt by those mothers who suffer from shy bowel syndrome.

A debriefing session will be held the following day sometime after the hamburger, hot chip and Coke lunch. This will be an opportunity for all mothers to express their remorse for what happened the night before and also have a good laugh. A two-hour sleep will follow.

Night two will provide all mothers with the opportunity to attend a "How To" workshop of their choice. Workshops include: How to DeBanana a School Bag, How to Lie to a School Librarian,

How to Clean the House (and Weed the Garden) in Five Minutes and How to Do an Undetectable Shoulder Charge.

Shots...oops sorry...spots will disappear quickly — so get in early!

Meeting closed 10.32pm.

Ma's Time

- *2 measures Jamaican rum*
- *juice of 1 lime*
- *½ measure Curaçao*
- *¼ measure orgeat syrup*
- *¼ measure sugar syrup with a couple of drops of vanilla extract*
- *mint for garnish*

Pour all ingredients into a cocktail shaker and fill with ice. Shake well for 10 seconds and strain into glass filled with crushed ice. Garnish with lime and a sprig of fresh mint.

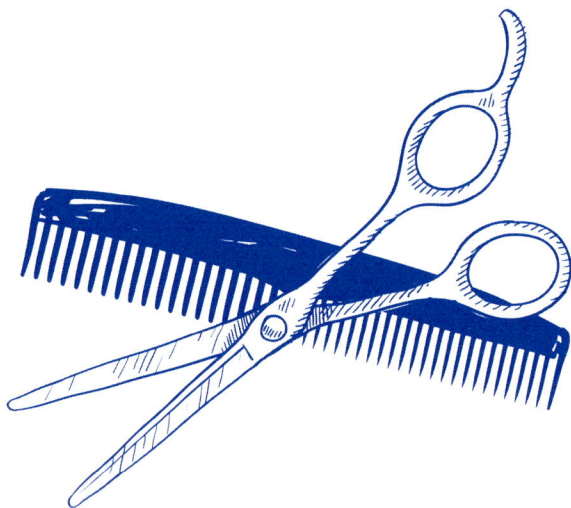

The Haircut

Last week I had a bad haircut. Now, I know they say the difference between a bad haircut and a good haircut is a week, but I came out looking like Donald Trump, so I don't think a week is going to make a whole lot of difference here.

My new 'do has forced me to cancel all social engagements for at least the next month, and it's also started me thinking about the whole hairdressing experience.

Hairdressers, I hope you appreciate the power of your position. As you reach for the scissors, do you realise that you hold the whole social diary of one person in your hands?

I have a feeling that the bald guy who cut my hair knew how powerful he was. There he was, scissors and combs jangling off the belt of his leather pants, constantly checking out his anorexic 16-year-old apprentice. He had the music up so loud that I was unable to decipher the odd little comments he threw at me.

"I'm gonna mash you like the ju-jubies."

Me, smiling and nodding, smiling and nodding. It was only when he took the black cloak off that I realised he was probably saying, "I'm gonna make you look like Judge Judy."

Speaking of the black cloak, isn't it time someone came up with a better idea to keep hair off you? I dare anyone to come forward and say they actually look good in one of those things.

Usually I arrive at a salon, confident and assertive. Half an hour later, after fracturing a couple of vertebrae getting my hair washed and looking like an extra from a swamp monsters movie with wet, straggly locks and that black cape wrapped too tightly around my neck, I am reduced to a passive, depressed being who will agree to anything to make herself look good.

One not-so-close-anymore friend actually told the truth when he saw the haircut. "Oh my god, what have you done? That haircut has aged you 10 years."

That was not a wise move. He will probably be coming out of hospital at around the same time as I will be able to tuck my front bits behind my ears, i.e., six months.

My advice to all is to lie. Keep it short and simple. "Oh, you've had a haircut, it really suits you." Don't embellish.

Try as they might, my children could not hide their embarrassment and no longer wanted me to drop them off or pick them up from school. I tried to look at the positives: at least this is one way of getting them to catch the bus to and from school. But I'm also not welcome at any school functions and, as luck would have it, the bad haircut happened the weekend before Education Week. Of course the school has decided to have a week full of cute songs and open classrooms but I have been told in no uncertain terms that I will not be welcome at any of these events. A quick thinking bad mother offered to film the performances and the classrooms for me so I don't miss out. I took her up on the offer and will watch my children via video link like I might if I was in jail.

In my confined state, I came up with the idea of starting a support group, SOBH — Survivors of Bad Haircuts. I imagine us sitting around reminiscing about the good old days when we could pull our hair back into a ponytail and planning devious ways of murdering our hairdressers. I already know how I am going to do in the bald guy. It's a foolproof plan involving a wash basin and a black cloak. Perhaps I might end up in jail after all.

My mother buried three husbands — and two of them were only napping.

Rita Rudner

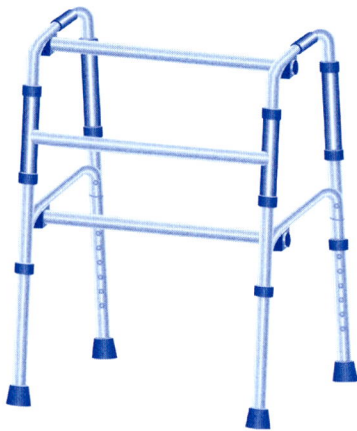

108

Nine Minutes

A sign outside the local beauticians alerting us that we only had eight weeks to get waxed before Santa comes down the chimney prompted a rash decision by a group of mothers to call an extraordinary meeting. A guest speaker, specially trained in PCCP (Prevention of Catastrophes from Christmases Past) was invited along. The minutes follow:

The guest speaker started by asking for a volunteer to talk about a catastrophe from a Christmas past so that we could dissect the incident and perhaps work out strategies to prevent its reoccurrence. A number of hands went up and one mother was chosen. She recounted last Christmas Day — a day where she'd had 10 too many champagnes and lost her own identity, preferring instead to introduce herself to relatives as "I am Pegasus — my name means horse." This was followed by a particularly raunchy rendition of the '70s classic complete with horse/saddle actions, and involving an elderly relative's walking frame. As a result a number of siblings are still not returning her calls.

As she spoke the guest speaker jotted down the incident in point form on a whiteboard. Champagne. Pegasus. Singing/dancing. Walking frame. And then asked us where we thought the mother had gone wrong.

One mother suggested that she probably should have chosen a different song — perhaps the Lionel Richie classic "Hello, is it me you're looking for?" might have been a better way of introducing herself. Another bad mother agreed that it wasn't a good song choice due to the number of names in the lyrics — Jeffery, John, Demetrius, Simon — she said she had enough trouble remembering her own husband's name.

The guest speaker stopped the discussion at that point and asked all mothers present to have a good look at the whiteboard to see if there was one word written there that, if removed, would have prevented the catastrophe in the first place.

A general murmur of "walking frame" rippled through the group. One mother asked if there had been any other props available. The mother in question thought for a moment before saying she hadn't really considered using anything else for the horse. In fact, she felt she had chosen the safest option because it was easy straddling height and it probably wouldn't topple over. All eyes diverted to the PCCP expert at this point who was forced to agree that, "Yes, if you needed to pretend that you were riding a horse, a walking frame was probably a safer option than a chair."

"What about this?" he said, stabbing his whiteboard marker vigorously at the word "champagne".

All mothers looked at their watches. It was a little early, but what the hell.

Meeting closed 10:34am.

Plants A Punch

- *3 measures dark Jamaican rum*
- *1 measure sugar syrup*
- *freshly squeezed lime juice*
- *3 dashes of bitters*
- *sprig of mint*

Combine ingredients in a tall glass and fill with crushed ice. Swish around until a frost forms on the outside of the glass. The ice will settle as you do this. Add more crushed ice if necessary. Garnish with a sprig of mint.

The Early Christmas Shopper

I spotted her across the shopping centre. She was easy to see. Long rolls of wrapping paper sticking out of her trolley and that damn smug look on her face that said, "I've finished all my shopping and now all I have to do is wrap."

I felt — as I do every year when I spot the first smug Christmas shopper — violent. I wanted to walk over and grab the rolls of paper and hit her around the head with them with enough force to knock her Christmas bell earrings out of her ear lobes.

I'm not normally like this. For most of the year, I'm fairly placid, but these smug shoppers seem to bring out my bad side.

I watched as she pushed her non-wobbly-wheel trolley through the shopping centre. She was headed to the food hall, probably to get the Christmas prawns, to take home and put in her freezer next to the pastry cases she had already prepared for the Christmas lunch entrée — the recipe for which she cut out of last year's Women's Weekly Festive Food special and kept in a safe place for 12 months.

In my mind's eye after she bought the prawns she headed to the car park to put them in an ice-filled esky in the boot of the car. She, of course, had arrived early and had the best car space in the place and now, out of the corner of her eye, she would have seen some blow-in slam on their brakes and put their blinker on while they did the bottom dance in their seat, delightedly shocked at how lucky they were to get such a great park.

But no. The smug Christmas shopper wasn't ready to leave yet. After she ensured that every little tiger prawn had found a snug place in the ice, she took an excruciating five minutes to close the boot, and then turned to the blow-in and shook her head, giving a "you're very silly for thinking you deserve a park like this" look. Then she wheeled her trolley back to the shopping centre to spend another hour or so picking up a couple of little trinkets in case someone unexpected turned up on Boxing Day.

As I watched I wanted to follow her and plan some sort of revenge. Secretly sneak something onto her to-do list that makes no sense at all, like "Buy present for K" and see how she reacted. But I didn't. I stopped myself — content in the fact that when Christmas Day arrives, I won't have to sit down and eat thawed eight-week-old prawns and open some gift she found on a half-price table in June.

All women become like their
mothers — that is their tragedy.
No man does. That is his.

Oscar Wilde

Ten Minutes

An extra extraordinary meeting of bad mothers was held yesterday afternoon (Christmas Day) to help one bad mother who'd had a completely disastrous day. She started by telling us that the day had started badly due to her eight year old being so frightened of Santa Claus that he'd stayed awake the whole night waiting for the big man in red to arrive. At five in the morning, with the presents still undelivered and she by now utterly exhausted, the bad mother had thrown her hands in the air and shouted "FOR GOD'S SAKE HE'S NOT EVEN REAL!", which of course woke the other child in the room and so began an hour-long sob fest. On hearing the wailing, the father of the children had come into the room, surveyed the psychological

catastrophe that the bad mother had created, shaken his head in disgust and retreated to the garage.

With ten relatives arriving in a couple of hours (his side), the bad mother had to do a complete renovation of the house in order to get it ready for what was a very tidy group of people. As she cleaned the kitchen, she realised with horror that she'd forgotten to put the cooked chickens she'd bought the day before in the fridge. She froze and looked around for what other food she might offer. But, despite the fridge being full to groaning point and the kitchen benches laden with all sorts of delicacies, the only alternative menu option she could come up with was honey sandwiches. At that point, the teenager of the house walked past eating a chicken leg for breakfast. She decided that she would use him as her guide. If he was OK by lunchtime, she would serve the chickens. She shoved them in the oven on low and kept cleaning.

When the relatives arrived (right on time), they were met at the door by a red-eyed three year old. "What's the matter with you?" the bad mother's very good mother-in-law asked.

"Santa's not real," said the three year old, bursting into tears.

"Who told you that?" asked the mother-in-law, giving the distraught child a hug.

"Mum," sobbed the three year old, pointing at the bad mother like she was in a line up.

The bad mother ducked for cover by pretending she needed to use the bathroom, but she was just beaten to it by the teenager, clutching his tummy and complaining of not feeling well. The bad mother returned to the kitchen to hushed comments and dagger stares.

"So great to have you all here!" she said, trying to sound genuine. "For lunch we have honey sandwiches or chicken and baked vegies. Which would you prefer?"

The relatives laughed nervously. Of course everyone wanted the chicken. She served it up, sent a mayday call out for an extra extraordinary meeting and got the hell out of there.

Meeting closed 11.45pm.

'Cos I'm not apologisin'

- *1 1/2 measures citrus-flavoured vodka*
- *1/2 measure Cointreau*
- *1/2 measure cranberry juice*
- *1/4 measure fresh lime juice*
- *glazed cherry for garnish*
- *orange twist*

Fill a cocktail shaker with ice. Add all
ingredients including the cherry and shake
well. Strain into a chilled cocktail glass
and garnish with orange twist. And stop
apologising.

Mothers Group Number Four

Since the birth of my children, I have been to more than my share of mothers groups. Let's see, there was the highly descriptive bodily fluids group, the really competitive height, weight and number of teeth group and the extremely vicious, almost carnivorous, man-hater group. Each time I left one, I'd swear I'd never go back to another and then someone would get in my ear with the routine about how my children needed to mix with other children or there was a very good chance they'd end up becoming a mass-murderer. And so now I'm in Mothers' Group Number Four and things are looking pretty good. We meet, weather permitting, outdoors, the mothers are really nice and to date there have been no number of teeth comparisons, no detailed nappy descriptions and men are generally regarded as more than just sperm donors.

For those of you feeling disillusioned with your mothers' group or if you've just left one and are wondering how to make a good start with the next — here are a few tips.

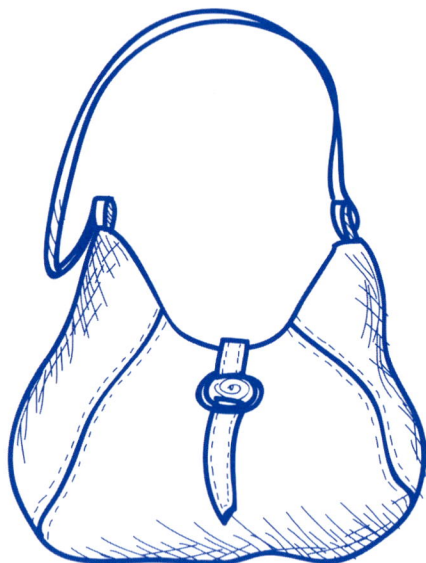

Firstly, labour stories are an inevitable part of any mothers' group. Make sure you have your labour story clear in your head…and then double it. If it took two hours for the anaesthetist to arrive with the epidural, make it four. Six stitches become twelve. One husband leaving the room to check the football score becomes one husband and his best mate leaving the hospital to check the score at the local pub. And so on. Let's face it — no one is going to be interested in your eight-hour, no-stitches, staff-were-a-dream story, so spice it up a little: it's allowed under the Delivery Suite Act. Over the years, to keep the stage, I've had to embellish quite a bit and my story now goes along the lines of going into labour eight thousand feet in the air, being taken up to First Class and having an emergency caesarian performed by a fellow traveller who just happened to be an expert in the field and then having the baby's cord cut by Kylie Minogue, who was so moved by the whole ordeal that she went back to her seat and penned the smash hit "I Should Be So Lucky".

Secondly, never, ever, divulge the contents of your mothers bag to other mothers, especially cupcake mothers. After child number two, a bad mother's bag will be filled with an assorted array of paraphernalia including a dozen or so half-eaten rusks, a couple of yogurts that Louis Pasteur would be happy to get his hands on, bottles of out-of-date Panadol, some unopenable hard-cover alphabet books with pages stuck together with mashed up banana, a collection of tupperware containers all containing sultanas and an assortment of chewed-up rice crackers. If you absolutely must open your bag at mothers' group, get in, retrieve what you need and then get out of there as quickly as you can.

And, finally, never ever lie about the behaviour of your child because sure as chips, the minute you say one thing, the child will do the complete opposite. For example, a particularly annoying mother in the highly descriptive bodily fluids group once asked me if my baby's bowel motions had been really runny since the change to formula. Just to get on this woman's nerves, I lied and said "No, she's been fine." Ten minutes later as I was holding my bonny bub, she had an explosion that would have done Mt Vesuvius proud.

By the way, have you seen those parents who, when asked if their child is sleeping through the night, glare at each other? They know full well that if they publicly reveal their newly discovered six-hour sleep span, they will spend the next two weeks reforging the track in the carpet that is only just starting to grow back.

Well! Mothers Group Number Four looks like it's for me. And, as I sit here gloating in the revelation that there is life after Mothers Groups One, Two and Three, I urge those of you presently trapped in an "Oh no — is it Thursday already?" situation, to pack up those extra-large mothers bags and start shopping around.

Neurotics build castles in
the air, psychotics live in them.
My mother cleans them.

Rita Rudner

Eleven Minutes

As a way of alleviating high stress levels, a decision was made to replace this month's bad mothers meeting with a yoga class. All bad mothers arrived on time at the local hall — one was carrying a deflated surfer plane that she'd retrieved from the garage in the hope it might pass as a yoga mat.

The instructor began by asking us all to go into child pose. Not familiar with this position, all bad mothers did their own interpretation: one stood hands on hips and bottom lip jutted

forward, another swung her arm vigorously to and fro, like she was slamming a door and another stormed around the room, arms folded, rolling her eyes. Once directed into the correct position by the instructor, all bad mothers took a deep breath and relaxed — who'd have thought a position named "child" could be so relaxing? — but of course this didn't last for long. "Come out of your child," said the instructor softly, "and I want you to go straight into seal." The bad mothers began to giggle. One left the room in a very hasty manner. Those remaining were instructed to shift from seal to barking seal — a move that prompted two other mothers to burst out laughing and quickly sprint from the room. From barking seal we went to sphinx and from sphinx we went to colicky baby. With every move, another bad mother had to quickly excuse herself to save embarrassment. Ten minutes into the class, only a few bad mothers remained, and they didn't last long once they were asked to go into cow face pose.

With the meeting now relocated to the amenities block, a discussion around pelvic floor exercises (PFEs) evolved, where all bad mothers confessed to not having done one PFE in their lives despite multiple pregnancies and constant bombardment from toilet door propaganda alerting us to the dangers of what might happen if we didn't do an internal workout 15 times a day.

"I mean, how ridiculous is that?" said one bad mother. "Working on muscles you can't even see? If I'm going to work out, I'd like to at least see the results."

Another bad mother piped in. "Imagine an aerobics class for internal muscles. The music would be blaring and everyone would just be standing there with a funny look on their face." All bad mothers burst out laughing as they pictured the scene. A decision was made to replace yoga with wine and all mothers adjourned to the local café for lunch where the most popular pose was "reclining mother with glass".

Meeting closed 2.47pm.

Tom Collins

This name can be replaced with that of any other male who might be annoying you at any given time.

- *2 measures gin*
- *juice of 1/2 lemon*
- *1 teaspoon fine sugar*
- *chilled soda water*

Pour gin into a glass. Add lemon and sugar and stir to dissolve sugar. Fill glass with large chunks of ice and top with chilled club soda. Drink quickly.

A Hell Of A Time

I have always been a firm believer in Jean-Paul Sartre's saying that "Hell is other people". Which is why I don't like going to places where there are other people — or lots of them, anyway. But then every so often an event comes along that is too good to miss — like when they bubble-wrapped half the Impressionist collection from the Musée d'Orsay in Paris, put it on a plane and brought it over to adorn the walls of the National Gallery in Canberra. This is the sort of event that will make me emerge from my cave and battle the inevitable crowds. It was too good to miss. I took a deep breath, doled the kids out for a night and booked some accommodation. I arrived feeling nervous.
I had read some reviews of the exhibition and there were many complaints about the long queues to get in. But it wasn't so bad. The time passed quickly and everyone was well-behaved. Within no time I'd handed in my entry ticket and was thinking that perhaps I had been a little harsh with other people.

I entered the exhibition feeling more relaxed than I had imagined — until a woman shouted: "YOU HAVE TO LOOK AT ALL THE PICTURES! EVERY SINGLE ONE! YOU CAN'T RUN AROUND LIKE A CRAZY THING!"

I looked around for who she might be screaming at. She grabbed a toddler by the arm. With his height and the number of people in the room, he would be lucky to catch a glimpse of the power sockets. I decided to further define Sartre's saying. "Hell is parents who take a two-year-old into a cultural mosh-pit and expect them to be interested."

I made my way over to Van Gogh's self portrait and was enjoying studying his use of colour until I was nudged by the man next to me.

"You see how it's all in the technique — you just keep smudging and the colours eventually join together." He wanted me to join in the discussion, but I had no reply. I was busy redefining Sartre's quote again. "Hell is experts."

As I moved through the gallery, the ''other people'' became more and more badly behaved. People with no peripheral vision. People in large groups with name tags on who stood in doorways talking about how pleasantly surprised they were with the Canberra weather and that they'd packed a lot of unnecessary jumpers. People who saw someone in a wheelchair and decided to do everything in their power to use that person to become a human obstacle path.

I retired to a seat in a corner and watched them all elbowing each other from room to room. As I sat, I wondered what Van Gogh would have thought of all this. A man who only sold one painting before his death, aged 37. A man who'd painted the beautiful *The Starry Night* because that was the view from his window at an asylum.

I think he would have said, "Let's get out of here." And that's what I did. I left the building, bought myself a glass of champagne and sat on the banks of Lake Burley Griffin to watch the sun set. Now that was heaven!

Twelve Minutes

A coincidental meeting of bad mothers was held last night when we all turned up one after the other at the local pub. After ordering and consuming an appropriate amount of wine, the bad mothers began to talk about just exactly what had unfolded which had caused a mass Sunday night exit from our homes.

The day, of course, had been Mother's Day. One bad mother reported that she felt she had started the day a lot better than past Mother's Days. She had feigned surprise at the arrival of breakfast in bed, despite the fact that she'd heard five items of crockery and glassware smash, instructed the six year old on how to switch on the kettle and told the four year old where the tea bags were kept.

She had then received, with much delight, the school-made Mother's Day gifts: a papier-mâché mouse pad made out of a collage of New Idea pictures (and featuring a large amount of Kardashian cleavage), and a pasta necklace to add to her already extensive collection.

It was at this point that the day began to go downhill. With the breakfast kitchen staff now clocked off and nowhere to be found, the bad mother spent an hour renovating the kitchen and was just about to do a stocktake of the crockery cupboard when she noticed water trickling from the laundry. She opened the door to find the room flooded and the washing machine lights in blink mode in an effort to get assistance. As she stepped into the room, she slipped on a lolly wrapper and, as she crashed to the floor, she whacked her elbow on the side of the machine. She landed flat on her back on the wet tiles where she lay for a period of time saying the same word over and over. No prizes given for guessing what the word was. The rescue team only arrived when they wandered in from the backyard wondering what was for lunch.

"Lunch!" she said. "Lunch! I'll tell you what's for lunch!" At this point her husband stepped in and said that maybe it was a good idea to retrieve the mother from the wet floor, put some new clothes on her and take her out for lunch. However, because there had been no prior planning, the bad mother was then taken to the only place in town that had a spare table — a venue she described as aspiring to be an old people's home for forty and fifty year olds.

Arriving home, and still trying to digest one of the most disgusting meals she'd ever eaten in her life, she was greeted by the dog, who presented her with a headless rat — a gesture that the children and husband found not only incredibly funny but also quite moving. It was at this point that the bad mother stood up and shouted, "I JUST WANT TO HAVE A REAL MOTHER'S DAY."

A proclamation that incensed family members as they felt that that was exactly the day she'd been given.

As the meeting progressed into the small hours, and each bad mother had a chance to recap their own series of disastrous events, we all had a good gut laugh and the realisation hit us that, yes, that was exactly the day we'd all just had — a real Mother's Day.

Meeting closed late.

Last Word

- *1 measure gin*
- *1 measure freshly squeezed lime juice*
- *1 measure Maraschino liqueur*
- *1 measure Chartreuse*

Combine ingredients in a cocktail shaker filled with ice. Shake it like you mean it for 10 seconds and then strain into a chilled cocktail glass.